THE
BENJI BOOM EFFECT

"An investment in knowledge always pays the best interest"

- Benjamin Franklin

THE

BENJI BOOM

EFFECT

Benji Boom

Lakeside InkPress

THE BENJI BOOM EFFECT

For information contact:
www.benjiboom.com

Cover Design by Lakeside InkPress Copyright © 2020
ISBN: 978-1-7331103-1-0 (paperback), 978-1-7331103-2-7 (e-book)
First Edition, 2020
10 9 8 7 6 5 4 3 2 1

To learn more

please visit

www.benjiboom.com

or

find us on social media

@BenjiBoomEffect

Instagram

Facebook

Twitter

YouTube

CONTENTS

Introduction.

WHAT IS THE BENJI BOOM EFFECT?

"A Penny Saved, Is A Penny Earned"
- Benjamin Franklin

Oh, I love that phrase! Hi, I'm Benji Boom, speaking to you as that $100 dollar bill you sometimes keep, and sometimes spend. I'll be your trusted guide over the pages of this book. My goal is to help you find a way to retire sooner with abundance, giving you peace of mind. You've worked hard for your money, now let it work for you.

Let's look again at the quote above. It's a simple phrase with a useful meaning. By not spending a penny, not only have you saved the penny, but you're up a penny, rather than down one. Simply put, it's just as useful to save money that you already have, as it is to earn more.

Of course a penny isn't worth much in today's modern world, so let's update it to inflation, shall we?

"A Benji Saved, Is A Benji <u>BOOMED</u>!"
- Benji Boom

We're talking $100 bills here! You're going to need many more of me to last into your retirement. That's where The Benji Boom Effect comes into play. We want to gather as much of me as you can.

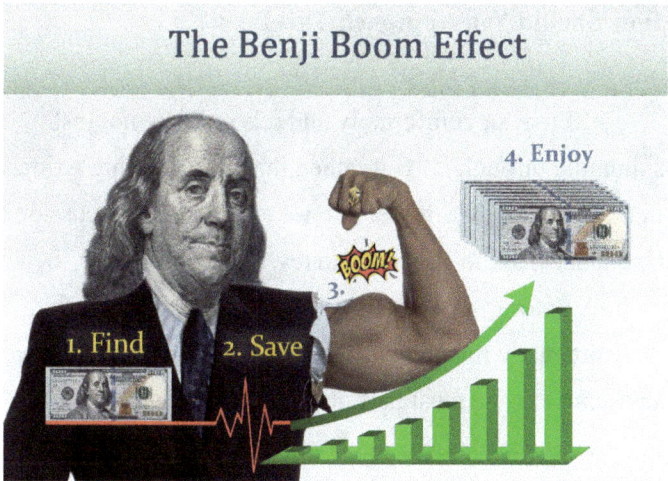

The Benji Boom Effect

To experience The Benji Boom Effect, you must follow these 4 simple steps:

1. Find
2. Save
3. BOOM!
4. Enjoy

Throughout this book, not only will we save the Benji's, we will grow them too. Safely and soundly. Every little Benji found will make your money count. Let's bring you closer to a fulfilling retirement. That is The Benji Boom Effect!

3

How Should You Approach This Book?

First, sit comfortably and relax. We're not just skimming through it. But rather, this book is being written in a way that makes it feel like we are having a discussion. One that eases the stress of money.

Before we go further, it is important to note, that there are many financial gurus with books that have many answers. For the most part, it is helpful reading, but a lot of these financial books get bogged down by unnecessary details with information catered to the masses.

This book is also being written to filter out the fluff, and focus on general concepts, rather than figures. That being said, there will be a few numbers and examples given, but the overall idea here is to understand the concepts, rather than studying and comparing charts.

By the same token, every person is unique with their own particular stream of income. What works for one person may not work for another. That is why you must use this book only as a general guide to reference ideas. This should not be used as legal advice, as each person's situation will be different. Please consult a certified professional for individualized advice. Or you can visit my website for more information-

www.benjiboom.com

WARM-UP: **DEFINE VALUE**

How does *VALUE* affect your life?

Before going full steam ahead, it is very important to understand yourself first. When I say the word VALUE, what does that mean to you? Some would say it measures their net worth. Others use the term to define obtained possessions.

Here, we are going to define Value as what is important in your life. Think about the priorities, principles, and ideas that serve as a standard for your life. We must explore and define these values first, before delving into the future of your money.

You want to skip all this pseudo-nonsense and get to the point? Then answer quick...

What would you do with $1 Million?

Many of you will stumble on this answer. Some of you already have $1 Million, but it's draining fast. Others of you want it, but don't understand how to get there. Many people will find themselves in a position where money leaves just as fast as it comes. The more you have, the harder it is to keep.

There is a better way. It begins with having a strong core of values. Together we must look within you to define these set of values, first. It will guide you to a higher quality of life.

Define and Understand.

So let's explore. What values define your life? Kindly write them down on the next page. Don't worry, you don't have to come up with too many! But I want you to come up with 4. Some of you will have more than that... please select your Top 4. Others of you might have less than 4. If that happens, and you're drawing a blank, then feel free to select any from my list below:

- Excitement
- Spirituality
- Time
- Growth
- Friendship
- Tradition

Also, please understand when we speak of value, I don't mean an activity or a possession. For example, "Golfing" is not a value. It is an activity. So when you say golf is important to you, think about what it gives you: Freedom, Relaxation, Discipline -- These are called values.

Here's another example. Sally is a fashionista who keeps up with all the current trends. She loves finding the finest clothes, jewelry, and accessories. But most important, she loves adding to her shoe collection. (Those heels are amazing!) She wants to write "Shopping" as a value. But it is not a value. It is an important activity she enjoys… so what does it give her? Curiosity, Fun, Adventure -- These are values.

Sally is also very open to sharing and expressing her mind. So much so, she is allowing me to share her 4 Values. Check them out:

1. Curiosity
2. Balance
3. Generosity
4. Wisdom

So now it's your turn,

take a minute to come up with your Top 4 Values.

(Take your time)... (This is important)...

(Remember... We're doing this for YOU!)

Now kindly write them down in each quadrant
on the next page.

YOUR CORE VALUES

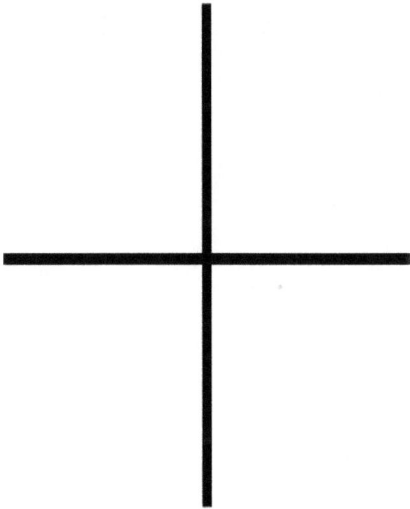

Thank you for doing this. You are already taking the first step. These values have now been defined and absorbed into the forefront of your mind. Soon, things in life will seem to subconsciously draw you to these values with no effort. This will guide you to a fulfilling life!

Lastly, I want you to take a look at Sally's Values:

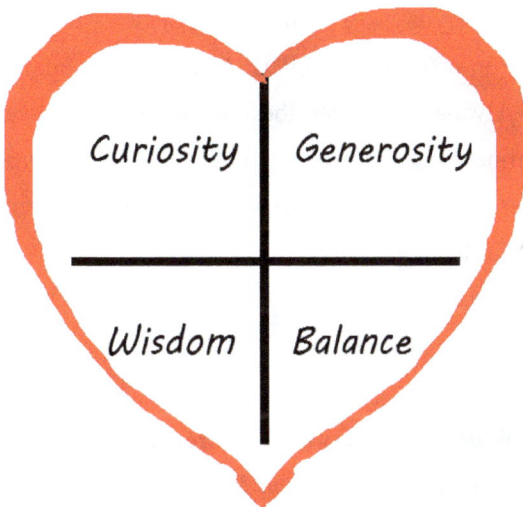

Curiosity   Generosity

Wisdom   Balance

Notice the heart I drew around it? We've helped Sally get to the *heart* of what defines her. Now I want you to go back to yours, and do the same thing. Kindly draw that heart around yours.

(Go ahead. I'll wait!)

Thank you for doing that. You are now welcome to tear your Page of Values out of this book (that's why I left its next page blank). Mount it up on a spot where you can see it everyday as a reminder to yourself. It can be on your mirror, office desk, bulletin board… anywhere.

Always remember, these values are at the heart of what defines you. It will help guide you to your purpose. This exercise we just did, is a warm-up to prepare our mindset for the main part of this book.

With your values now defined, we are now ready to implement The Benji Boom Effect! Let's begin...

STEP 1: FIND

The Benji Boom Effect

1. Find

Hiding In Plain Sight

That's right, your Benji's are hiding in plain sight.
Step 1 of The Benji Boom Effect involves taking off the
blinds that shield you from money already in your pocket.
It's there, you just don't know it yet.

Understanding Opportunity Cost

In life, so much money will flow through your
hands, but it's what you do with it that counts. Every
dollar matters, because it's an opportunity to grow it into
many Benji's. It is up to you, to make sound decisions so
that you maximize the potential growth of every dollar.

Imagine your flow of money as water going into buckets…

In the financial industry, many planners take a popular approach known as the 3-Bucket Strategy. If you're not familiar with it, that's okay. We will review a variation of this approach to reach your goals. Each bucket coincides with each step of The Benji Boom Effect.

Bucket #1 -- Taxable Bucket

This is your most used bucket, because every year you fill it up with income sources. It is everything that you earn: Salary, Wages, 1099, W-2, Rental Income, Certificate of Deposit, or any other income stream.

Unfortunately, there are major leaks in this bucket. One is in the form of taxes, the most popular being federal and state income tax. Even more holes occur in the FICA tax taken out of your paycheck to pay for Social Security and Medicare.

$ Income Source $

Taxable Bucket

Taxes
Bills

Expenses
Luxury/Travel

While these leaks occur, you begin to notice another big one… LOSSES! It comes in many forms. Your cost of living is necessary to sustain you. Expenses form in maintaining your lifestyle. Bills need to be paid to keep going. Meanwhile, travel & luxury are pleasures that you deserve.

Just when you think you've found all the leaks, another one forms. Now you have to pay off loans, mortgages and credit cards. Before you know it, there's hardly any water left in the bucket to move into your retirement bucket.

Fortunately, you're still earning so you put more water in the bucket, only to have the leaks drain it down. Yet, you still keep doing this over and over, every year.

When will it end? If you remain stuck in this approach, you won't have much to enjoy in retirement. Your quality of living will be reduced. Do you want to live this way?

There's a solution: PLUG THE HOLES! Reduce the taxes, curb wasteful spending, and refinance any debts. These are just a few ideas which we will explore later, but taking these steps will slow the bucket from draining out.

Find The Leaks

The best way to plug the holes is to plan first. What are the leaks? Throughout life, you will obtain money through various channels in career, investments and possible inheritance. All of these will be put to the test to see how well it remains in your bucket.

So where are your leaks? They come in many forms. It is up to you to find them, and seal them, so that you can enjoy your bucket. Below is a list of common leaks we must seal in our Bucket of Wealth:

- *Taxes* - understand the government's rules, then reduce
- *Loans/Mortgage* - reduce monthly payment
- *Credit Card Debt* - end it and avoid, so that your debt avoids interest
- *Bad Life Insurance* - reevaluate how your plan fits you
- *Car Insurance* - lower monthly premium to maximize savings
- *IRA/401k* - yes, it's tax-deferred, but why risk a higher tax on a higher income later?
- *Education* - again, reduce the cost of debt so that your money remains with you
- *Other Expenses* - what other areas can you curb so that your money grows with you?

Please, Not That "Cup Of Coffee" Example Again!

(*Sigh*) Yes, by now you've already heard this famous example. But it drives a very good point that we'll briefly explore. For those of you who have not heard it yet, here it is:

Every morning you need that latte before work. Let's say that latte at your local coffee shop costs you $5. Multiplied by 5 days, it comes to $25/week on morning lattes. Over 4 weeks, that translates to $100/month. Now multiply it by 12 months and you've spent $1,200/year on lattes (calculated over 48 working weeks/year).

$5 Latte
x 5 days
_____
$25/week ⟶

$25/week
x 4 weeks
_____
$100/month

$100/month
x 12 months
_____
$1,200/year spent on Lattes

Obviously you don't want to give up lattes, so what's the solution? There is one. What if you make them at home before work? It would cost you ONLY 50 cents per cup. That's $2.50/week, $10/month, and $120/year - for that latte at home. It saves you $1,080/year. Let's say you do this for the next 30 years and put those yearly savings into a fund growing at 6-8%. That could turn into an extra $100,000 in your pocket just by changing how you get a latte. An extra $100,000 would be nice, right?

$0.50 Latte $2.50/week

x   5 days   x   4 weeks

$2.50/week ⟶ $10.00/month

$10/month

x 12 months

$120/year spent on Home Lattes

↓

$1,200/year Outside Latte

- 120/year Home Latte

$1,080 saved on Latte expense

$1,080/yearly saving

x 30 years

$32,400 Total Savings

↓ growth @ 6-8%

approx. ~ $100,000 Extra For You

Food For Thought

What other areas in your bucket can be saved? It is up to you to evaluate your expenses and find where else you can patch up leaks.

Another example is in food. It is easy to eat outside food, but nothing beats a healthy home-cooked meal. If you find yourself relying on outside food too many times a week, then you have found another leak in your bucket that can be curbed. It's okay to enjoy dining out, but moderation is key.

Take the example of my friends, Eric and Diane, who love dining out. A little tweak in their weekly habits changed their lives.

Eric & Diane BEFORE

Dine Out 2x a week	$80/week
Order In 3x a week	$60/week
TOTAL	$140/week
	$7,280/year

Eric & Diane AFTER

Dine Out 1x a week	$40/week
Order In 2x a week	$40/week
TOTAL	$80/week
	$4,160/year

$7,280 – $4,160 = $3,120 Saved Yearly

Car Insurance Overlooked

Another savvy friend named Courtney, plugged a leak by looking into her car insurance payments. Upon first examining, she found her premium payments were $3,000/year on a $500 deductible. It dawned on her that she is wasting money insuring something that depreciates significantly in value every year. She's a good driver. The only people who benefit are the car insurance companies.

In a smart move, she adjusted her car insurance plan by increasing the deductible to $2,000. This decreased her premium payments from $3,000/year to $1,500/year. By putting the savings of an extra $1,500/year in a fund, over 30 years at 6-8% interest growth, it gave her an extra $100,000. Needless to say, this added to her quality of life.

Deductible		Premium
$500	→	$3,000
↓		↓
$2,000	→	$1,500

$1,500/yearly saving

x 30 years

$45,000 Total Savings

↓ growth @ 6-8%

approx. ~ $100,000 Extra For You

Would you be happy with an extra $100,000? Of course! All these areas that we look into, is your Bucket of Wealth. We are simply plugging the leaks so that your money stays with you and grows safely.

Do You Like Apples?

Let's say I give you 2 apples, one in each hand. But now I take one away. What have you lost?

You have lost an apple, correct?

NO! What if I say you've lost more?? That apple has seeds that can grow into an apple tree. That apple tree has apples, that can grow more trees. And those trees can become orchards. Likewise, we are keeping the money you are leaking, so that we can replant its seeds to grow into apple trees that together, form vast orchards in your wealth. *How do you like them apples?*

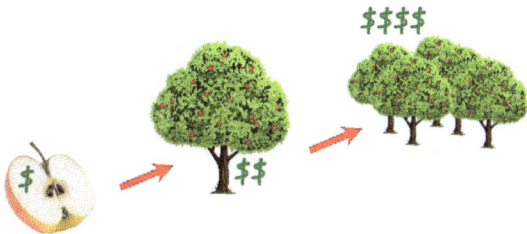

Change Your Financial Diet

Essentially, we are improving the health of your wealth by implementing better financial choices. Fixing the leaks will help maximize the value of every dollar so that you can grow them into many Benji's .

Now is the time to start this financial diet. Eliminate bad spending habits, and minimize unnecessary expenses. By sticking to this mindset, you will ***FIND*** extra money that was always with you.

Gather All Your Benji's

There are many ways to fix the leaks. Earlier on, we pointed to a few areas. We want to keep the Benji's with you so that you do not lose any money unaware.

Remember some of the examples from earlier:

1. Making more coffee at home
2. Eating outside food a little less
3. Reducing premiums on auto insurance

By making some of these simple changes, you can save and grow more Benji's without compromising your lifestyle. These 3 savings combined, could give you an extra $4,000/year. Over a 30-year period that's $120,000. If you let that grow in a fund at a 6-8% growth, it could become $500,000. Can you live better with an extra $500,000? Of course!

1. More home coffee $1,000
2. Less outside food $2,000
3. Reduce car insurance   + $1,000
                                        $4,000 yearly saving

$4,000/yearly saving
x 30 years
$120,000 Total Savings

growth @ 6-8%

approx. ~ $500,000 Extra For You

Let's take a look at a couple more areas…

Mortgage

When it comes to your house mortgage, there are many choices. Each individual case is different, so we'll take a basic approach. Let's assume you have a 15-year mortgage at a fixed rate of 4%. Your monthly payments are $2,100. Seems to be the best option as many people will say that you save more on interest over a 15-year mortgage rather than a 30-year mortgage. This is true.

However, what if we do a 30-year mortgage instead? Let's say your monthly payment reduces down to $1,400. Now you have an extra $700/month available. Some would argue that's a bad choice because even though you've lowered your monthly payment, you are paying more in interest overall.

That shouldn't matter to you because you have the power of The Benji Boom Effect. By putting that extra money into a fund, you are growing it over that same 30-year period which will offset a portion of the interest paid.

On top of that, there is a *Mortgage Interest Deduction* you can take advantage of for your tax savings. This means more Benji's saved in taxes, which you can grow! Most of you will qualify if your home loan follows a few parameters. The basic idea being, that the interest paid on your loan can be deducted.

In general terms, deductible mortgage interest is any interest you pay on a home loan used to purchase, build, or improve your home (or second home). The major update to the rule is that from 2018 onward, where your loan(s) must be limited to $750,000 to take deductions. There are more rules, but this is the general overview. If you qualify, then deduct the total interest you pay for these loans from your taxable income.

Definitely look into your mortgage if you haven't yet. You could lower the overall cost of interest simply by shifting the Benji's toward a fund that grows. You have two ways of doing this:

1. 30-Year Mortgage -- Lowers monthly payments, which frees up money to grow in a safe fund.
2. Mortgage Interest Deduction -- Allows extra tax-savings, which you can also grow in a safe fund.

* For more information on mortgages, check out www.mortgagecalculator.org

** The "fund" is actually in your Bucket #3, to be later discussed in this book. For now we're focusing on <u>finding</u> your Benji's... Keep reading!

Groceries

Each person and every family is unique. You know yourself better than anyone when it comes to behavior and preferences. So rather than tell you how to save money, we'll only review some general suggestions.

The goal here, is to not overkill on changing your behavior, but maybe we can find areas where you save $100/month. This would grow to an extra $1,200/year which becomes $36,000 over 30 years, saved on groceries. Put that into a fund, and you could grow another extra $100,000 for your retirement just on minor changes.

Here are a few popular suggestions:

1. *Coupons* - They add up. Everyone knows this, but keep track of them.
2. *Generic is good* – With medications, generic vs brand name drugs can save you money. A great example is Store Brand vs Tylenol/Advil. Same medicine, less cost. Look for areas where you don't need to compromise on quality when choosing lesser brands. Other examples: batteries, gasoline, paper towels, spices, and more.
3. *Visit the pantry* - Curb shopping around what you already have, so nothing gets wasted.

4. *Avoid pre-cut produce* - They stay fresh less longer, cost more & you get less for what you buy.

5. *No meat, 1 day per week* - Meat is expensive. If you eat it, try giving it up once a week. There are so many tasty vegetarian recipes. And it could save you $30/month.

6. *Finish leftovers* - Make leftovers a priority and you'll save money.

7. *Store food properly* - Again, don't waste food. Make it last and finish what you have.

8. *Eat Healthy* - Save money eating more fruits/vegetables instead of processed food. It will also improve your well-being which affects long-term health, and could help reduce medical bills if you remain healthier.

9. *Figure it out* - Review every few months & adjust, to maintain at least $50-$100/month in savings. Only you know what works best for you.

Keep in mind we are looking for simple changes here. Nothing drastic is needed, because this is just a portion of the overall strategy to get to a better retirement. It is most important that you remain happy in the present without adding stress.

Many financial planners try to cut money where you spend on luxury and lifestyle. We don't want to focus on that. We'd rather look to other areas in your overall strategy to find the extra money that you didn't know you have. That's why we focus on minimal changes to keep your Benji's, rather than a major cut to your lifestyle. Simply put, avoid unnecessary losses.

Avoid Unnecessary Taxes

Ugh… TAXES! Nobody likes them, except the government, but it goes without saying… Pay your taxes. They fund programs that keep society running. We are all in this together to fund the necessities of our civilization.

That being said, don't pay more than what is necessary. Is it fair that people like Warren Buffet pay a lower tax rate than his secretary? How about the fact that Amazon paid ZERO federal taxes in 2018?

Did you know that for the first time in a century, in 2018, the 400 wealthiest American families paid a lower tax than the middle class? This, according to a study by two esteemed economists, Emmanuel Saez and Gabriel Zucman.[1] We've all heard these and other similar stories.

---

1 Emmanuel Saez and Gabriel Zucman, *The Triumph Of Injustice* (W.W. Norton & Company; 2019)

What most of these people in this small club are doing, is keeping what the government allows them to keep.

You can do that too. What most people don't understand, or are unaware of, is how to do it. But before we explore this, please, please, please… do not become greedy. Countless wealthy people have found themselves in trouble with the IRS because of greed. Don't become one of them. The government is a partner giving you a chance to keep some of your money. It allows for you to take advantage of this, unless you cheat the system.

Taxes Are Amazing!

No, I'm not high. I know it sounds crazy, but right now it's absolutely true! Despite the unprecedented deficit growing over $26 Trillion (as of this writing), the Government is gifting you some more money in the form of lower taxes. Rather than increase taxes and decrease spending, it is doing the exact opposite.

In 2017, Congress passed the Tax Cut and Jobs Act, effective as of January 1, 2018. A sunset clause was built into this bill where this will last for 8 years. This means on January 1, 2026 taxes can rise back up to pre-2018 levels.

The good news is, you have a lot to gain in the

short-term, despite Uncle Sam's risky bet. Let's take a look at the tax charts on the next page. For those who do not understand the structure: different portions of your Earned Income is taxed at a certain percentage, as the amount of your Earned Income increases every level.

Take notice of the area where the tax rates are lower. Some of you will be saving a few thousand dollars based on this structure, which favors incomes over $100,000. It benefits you to take advantage of this extra money coming back to you by growing it in a fund.

Single Filers

2017 Tax Bracket	Taxable Income
39.6%	$418,400
35%	$416,700
33%	
	$191,650
28%	$91,900
25%	
15%	$37,950
10%	$9,325
	$0

2018-2026 Tax Bracket	Taxable Income
37%	$500,000
35%	
	$200,000
32%	$157,500
24%	
	$82,500
22%	
12%	$38,700
10%	$9,525
	$0

Married Filers Jointly

2017 Tax Bracket	Taxable Income
39.6%	$470,700
35%	$416,700
33%	
	$233,350
28%	$153,100
25%	
15%	$75,900
10%	$18,650
	$0

2018-2026 Tax Bracket	Taxable Income
37%	$600,000
35%	
	$400,000
32%	$315,000
24%	
	$165,000
22%	
12%	$77,400
10%	$19,050
	$0

Meanwhile, keep in mind that though this tax structure is in effect till 2026, the government can shift its rules in the coming years. As of writing this book, we are still in the Trump era. What happens next is up to the people. Whichever way Congress shifts politically, it most likely won't change the tax rates much if they're concerned about holding office. Therefore, you could have a bonus of a few years until 2026 when this tax structure is due to end. Either way, take advantage now of the money the government gives back to you.

Fill In Your Tax Rate

Present Year	
Next Year	
Year 2026	
Year 2027	

*check www.irs.gov for updated tax rate

Where To Begin?

That's easy. Find a good certified accountant who is up-to-date on the Tax Codes and Regulations. This person will be your guide to help you understand necessary write-offs. Ask around your network of people you trust, and soon you'll have a good accountant to partner with (if you don't have one already).

With your Benji's now found, we can move to Step 2! Let's do this...

STEP 2: SAVE

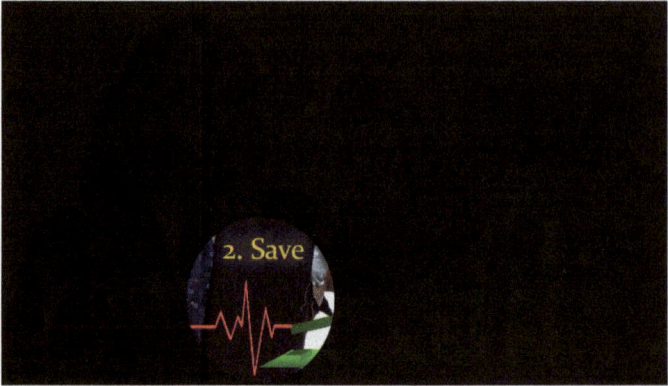

The Benji Boom Effect

2. Save

Don't Just Save It... SAVE IT!

We found our extra money by changing our Financial Diet in Step 1. Now in Step 2, we can implement a new routine that reshapes our wealth to last longer. Just like going to the gym in the first week, we are going to make big changes to what we've done in the past.

In fact, we're not just going to save it... we're going to ***SAVE IT*** from ineffective investments we thought were working for us. Just like how one would think he's doing everything right in diet and exercise, when all along his health still gets worse. Let's correct that issue.

Either you walk your Benji's down this sluggish path that goes up and down, resembling the EKG pulse...

or we can implement a more effective routine that stabilizes and increases the health of your wealth. Which would you rather do? Let's save it from more leaking.

Bucket #2 -- Tax-Deferred Bucket

Tax-Deferred Bucket

Income Sources

TAX Deferred

Pay Tax Later
IRA, 401(k), Defined Benefit Plan
Bottom Falls Out If Stock Market Crashes

Many times, a CPA or Planner will advise you to move some extra Benji's from Bucket #1 to a Bucket #2 that is *Tax-Deferred*. This is money that hasn't been taxed yet, which you are investing into an account that will grow. Then you pay the tax at a later point in time. Simply stated, you are postponing taxes on this money to a later point in time.

Some examples of these accounts are your IRAs (Individual Retirement Account). The 401(k) is the most popular. Others of you might have a Defined Benefit Plan. They all share the same characteristics:

1. Only "earned income" can be put into this account (typically wages/salary). Rental income DOES NOT count.

2. Limitations on how much you put in, per year.

(based on 2020)

IRA	$6,000/$7,000 (if age 50+)
401(k)	$19,500
SEP IRA	$57,000 or 25% of wages
Defined Benefit Plan	$230,000

3. Restriction on withdrawals.
    A. If you take money out before Age 59½
        ○ PAY INCOME TAX
        ○ PAY AN EXTRA 10% PENALTY
    B. If you don't take Required Minimum Distribution after Age 72
        ○ PAY 40% INCOME TAX
        ○ PAY AN EXTRA 50% PENALTY

   * *It is your responsibility to know this. The Government will enforce it.*

Don't mistake "tax-deferred" as tax savings. Let's assume you put $18,000/year into your 401(k) and you're currently in a 20% tax bracket. That's $3,600 that you're not giving to Uncle Sam. Many people fool themselves believing this is $3,600 saved, when in reality all they've done is postpone paying Uncle Sam his share.

Now let's fast forward to a later point in time, where that $18,000/year grows to $1.8 Million! Nice growth, but before you can enjoy that money you must pay Uncle Sam. Guess what? At this point, you will be in a higher tax bracket too because you've grown it to $1.8 Million. Who knows what it will be in the future, but let's assume a 40% tax bracket, as a result of this growth. Would you rather:

Pay 20% tax right now on $18,000?

-or-

Pay 40% tax later on $1.8 Million?

Seems pretty obvious how vulnerable this bucket has become. The crazy part is that it also performs to the stock market. Your $1.8 Million Account can be performing robustly, but if suddenly the market goes into a recession and loses 50%... you lose $900,000; emptied directly out the bottom of the bucket you entrusted.

Remember these 3 important rules:

1. If you lose, the Government won't put money back.
2. When you lose, it's YOUR money.
3. When you make money, the Government decides how much it will take.

Retirement Accounts In This Bucket

During your lifetime, most of you will likely come across two types of retirement accounts in this bucket.

1. *Employer Sponsored* -- from your company
2. *Individual Plan* -- from yourself

Let's take a brief look into the most famous one:

Play The 401(k)?

The 401(k), an employer sponsored plan, is well known and most popular, as most employers offer this to their employees. The name itself is derived from a section of tax law that labels it as a self-directed plan. Simply stated, the employer gives the plan and the employee controls it. This gives full control for the employee to participate in the plan, decide how much to contribute, and where to invest the money.

With that being said, it is your responsibility to see if your company offers a 401(k). If so, then it is on you to sign up for it according to company policy. Some may require you to be employed a minimum 6 months before signing up for one. Just don't assume that a 401(k) is automatic upon employment. It is on you to ask for it.

For those employed by a non-profit, you will have a similar plan called a 401(b).

Pay The 401(k)

First, understand what a 401(k) actually does. Most plans will invest across mutual funds composed of stocks, bonds, and money market investments. These investments tend to become conservative as you reach retirement. So you save and invest a piece of your paycheck before taxes are taken out. Taxes aren't paid until the money is withdrawn from the account after age 59½. If you withdraw before that, the money will both be taxed and subject to a 10% penalty, paid to the government. In short, avoid early withdrawal.

Your employer will have an overseer that represents the company handling your plan. They will give you updates on performance and manage requests. They act as a bridge to the decisions you make.

You can contribute up to $19,000/year to your 401(k) in 2019. If you're aged 50 or over, the limit is $25,000/year. Some employers will offer to match your yearly contribution. The employer match that you receive does not count towards this limit. Understand that the government updates the rules on contribution limits. It is up to you to check on this every year.

So how much should you contribute? If you are going to participate in this plan, then consider only contributing up to the maximum your employer will match. It is free money for you that goes toward your growth.

Why would the employer give you free money? The company benefits in two ways. First, it helps retain employees in a competitive job market. Second, they get to count this money as tax write-offs. Either way, you benefit by receiving free money growing for you.

Pray For The 401(k)

> *Wait, what?*
> *That doesn't sound promising.*
> *Pray for my 401(k)?*

Yes, I'm telling you to pray for it. Here's why:

You're at the mercy of the market

Many retirement planners will say the market will give you a 7% annual return, some going as high as 10% a year. That may be true when measuring over the last century, but when you look over the past 20 years, you could argue annual growth is less than 1% when adjusted for inflation. Some will counter by pointing to the great growth between 2009-2019. In good times, that is great, but let's not forget the market will go down at some point, and your losses aren't protected. Your 401(k) is a long-term investment, and not just the past 10 years of growth.

You're at the mercy of the manager

Let's say you start a business with a partner. You put up 100% of the capital and your partner puts in zero.

No matter how the business runs, your partner collects a yearly fee regardless of you making a profit or loss. Is that a fair deal? That's what is happening every year that you keep this partnership with your 401(k) manager, and there's no guarantee in the market.

You're at the mercy of the padlock

What happens in an emergency and you need to access funds? This money is not liquid. The money in your 401(k) is locked in. You do not get the keys until age 59½. If you withdraw funds before that, you face a tax *plus* a 10% penalty, paid to the government. Even taking a limited loan with interest may sound safe, but should you leave your job, you could be forced to pay the outstanding loan within 60 days.

You're at the mercy of Uncle Sam

He's that Uncle you don't enjoy, but can't live without. There are a couple tax issues to consider. First, the estate tax. When it comes to the end of a person's life, some will leave a pile of money in their 401(k) to be passed on to their beneficiary. But without a proper strategy planned, the government will grab a chunk by taking an income tax and a huge estate tax, if it qualifies.

Second, the 401(k) is tax-deferred, which means you take out pre-tax dollars from your paycheck to fund your plan. It sounds great, because that's extra money working for you now, while you pay taxes later, when you receive distributions from it after age 59½.

But here's the catch... when that time comes to take distributions from your 401(k), you can be sitting on a bigger pile of money subject to a higher tax rate. Do you think taxes will remain at the current rates in the future?

Hello, This Is Your Morning Wake Up Call

Sorry, let's not alarm you too much, but there is a serious case to be made for your future when it comes to taxes. As I write this book, I can tell you that we are in one of the best eras in the history of federal income tax rates. They are still historically low since the 1980s, allowing you to do more with your dollars. You might be thinking, *that's crazy to say they're low.*

Now what if I told you that from 1936-1981, the top federal income tax rate never went below 70%... Don't believe me? Some of you younger people reading this weren't even alive. Check out the chart:

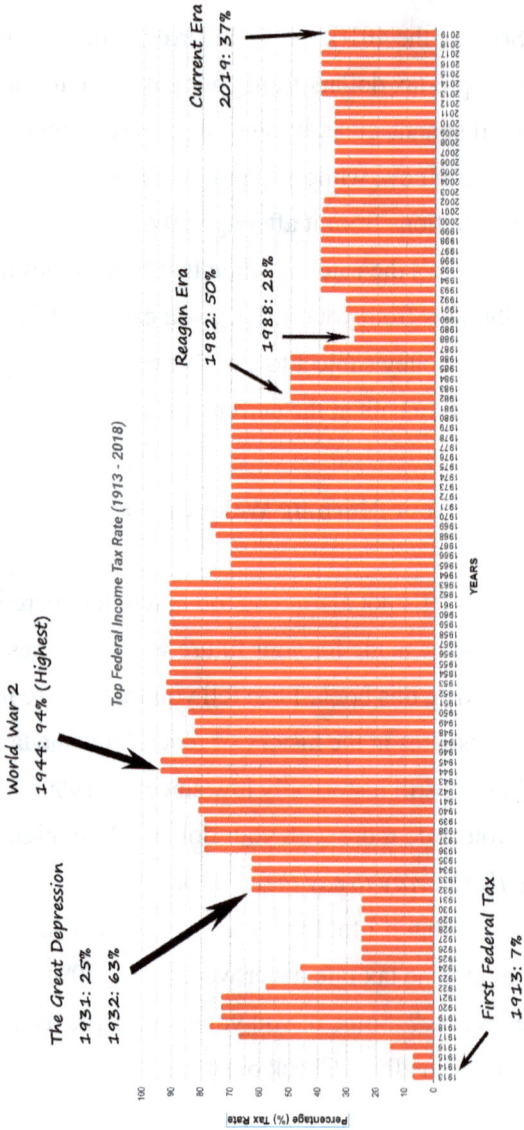

Top Federal Income Tax Rate (1913 - 2018)

World War 2
1944: 94% (Highest)

The Great Depression
1931: 25%
1932: 63%

First Federal Tax
1913: 7%

Reagan Era
1982: 50%

1988: 28%

Current Era
2019: 37%

Percentage (%) Tax Rate

YEARS

Who's Going To Get US Out?

There is a serious problem in America with our growing debt. Midway through the year 2020, we are past $26 Trillion in debt. If our government remains this careless, the debt will skyrocket even further. Eventually it will have to cover these enormous debts. Check out www.usdebtclock.org for a live update. You will see the national debt in the upper left hand corner.

How Did We Get Here?

It is important to understand how social security and medicare affects us. Both these programs are adding huge problems to our debt, but they are important and necessary for our society.

Back in 1935, Social Security was implemented into law. It was a stable program that gave retirees money after age 65. Back in those days life expectancy was around age 62. Most didn't live long enough to rely on Social Security, and even those that made it past 65 only lasted a few years on it. It was a great program for the government as an insurance against the few people who lived longer.

So what happened? After World War II, the Baby

Boomers entered our world. This generation made less babies than their previous, which meant fewer workers contributing money to the Social Security program.

On top of that, advancement in modern medicine has put a strain on Medicare. Life expectancy has gone up to age 78. With more people living longer, the costs are increasing to higher levels every year.

Over the next 10 years, most Baby Boomers will retire, which means more money needed from the taxpayer to pay for the biggest generation living in America. With an ever-shrinking workforce, how will the government generate enough revenue to pay for this aging population?

Go back to www.usdebtclock.org and in the second row, on the top left, you will see the two largest budget items are Medicare and Social Security. How big is it? Write it down in the chart below for perspective:

	Medicare	Social Security
Today		
5 Years Later		
10 Years Later		

Seriously, Who's Going To Get _US_ Out?

Well, the government can't pay for it. You are paying your taxes. And we've borrowed ourselves into debt to pay for our recent wars. Economic growth exists, but it isn't keeping up with our debt. So in the future, when the debt blows up to even more astronomical proportions, where do you think the government will most likely go for the money?

That's right, you the taxpayer! But you're already paying taxes, surely they can't ask for more. Or can they? Remember that graph earlier? They won't come for the poor, they barely have any money. You may not have it now either, but guess what? There's your 401(k) and countless others waiting to be taxed years from now, after age 59½.

Remember the example I gave you earlier about your 401(k) Manager being a business partner who collects fees? Well now you can add Uncle Sam as a third partner you forgot about, because he will collect taxes when the time comes. At anytime he can decide the new tax rate. Don't you think there's a high likelihood of higher tax rates in the future based on our government's current spending?

And you will oblige Uncle Sam, by law.

Change The Pulse

Now do you understand why we use an EKG pulse to define this chapter? We've brought the lost Benji's back to life, but this type of pulse is only normal for our human heart. When it comes to the heart of your money, we throw them into the stock market hoping for big gains, when all along it looks like this... going up and down.

Right now everything seems great in the stock market, but don't you think there's a recession looming? History will say it will happen in order for the market to correct itself. Do you want to be like one of those people who spent years putting earned money in the stock market, only to retire with nothing when the market crashed in 2009? What a risky way to live.

Despite saying all this, some will still go for a 401(k) because it has been ingrained into our psyche.

You'll even hear people brag about how well their plan is going or how they struck it big on a particular stock. What you'll never hear though, are the periods of loss or the other countless stocks that performed poorly. It goes without saying, other people's success has no bearing on you. Focus only on your personal growth.

The good news…
there's still time to choose a safer path.

STEP 3: BOOM!

The Benji Boom Effect

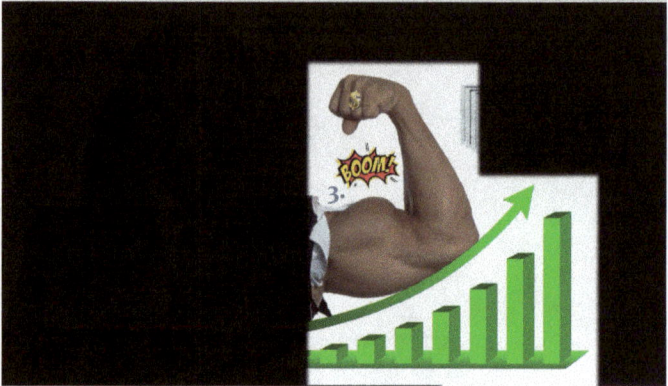

BOOM!

Do you have the patience and commitment to let your money BOOM? To build the Benji's, it requires a slow and steady pace, just like lifting weights in the gym. Building muscle doesn't happen overnight. Likewise we need to approach this with ease as the health of our wealth grows immensely.

Now that we saved your Benji's from the dreaded Tax-Deferred Bucket, we can place them into a safer alternative where it can BOOM! Is there another bucket that can safely do this? Of course!

Bucket #3 -- Tax-Free Bucket

Welcome to America's best bucket. You can let your money grow here TAX-FREE! There's no catch. Just pay taxes upfront, then put the money in, and watch it grow... TAX-FREE! It's not a trick. This really exists. So why aren't you taking advantage of this option?

Many Americans only fill the first two buckets. Barely a handful of people will even look into the realm of what this third bucket offers:

1. Your money grows TAX-FREE
2. All withdrawals are TAX-FREE
3. This bucket is Asset-Protected

If you're skeptical of this bucket, then let's take a quick look at what you're missing out on:

ROTH IRA

The Roth IRA is a Tax-Free retirement account unique from all the other Tax-Deferred IRAs. Why? Because it's TAX-FREE!! The government puts stringent limitations on this type of account. This can only mean one thing... It must be too much of a good thing, if the government strictly limits what you put into a Roth IRA.

First, you must make less than $193,000/year if you file jointly as a couple. For those who are single, you must earn less than $122,000/year to qualify for this account.

The second limit, is in yearly contributions. If you're younger than 50, then the maximum contribution is $6,000/year. Those older than 50 are allowed to contribute a maximum $7,000/year.

LIMITATIONS
ROTH IRA

Couple	Earn less than $193,000/year
Single	Earn less than $122,000/year
Under 50	Max. Contribution: $6,000/year
Over 50	Max. Contribution: $7,000/year

Only earned income can be used to fund this account, which means you have to be working somewhere and earning a paycheck in order to contribute to a Roth IRA. Should you need to withdraw any money before age 59½, then the funds contributed are available without penalty (because you already paid taxes before investing). However, any funds taken from the growth will be subject to taxes and penalties.

Verdict: It's great to have Tax-Free growth, but it comes with significant limitations. Should you qualify, then consider investing in a Roth IRA.

But what else is available in the Tax-Free Bucket? Turn the page…

LIFE INSURANCE

Imagine a Roth IRA on steroids! A place to put your money with no limitation on how much you contribute and no limitation on your income. This money grows in Life Insurance through its Cash Value in 3 ways:

1. *Conservative Portfolio* - A safe and consistent route, but gives you low returns
2. *Stock Market* - You can attain high returns, but also risk big losses
3. *Index* - Your money accumulates based on the growth of a group of stocks. The index funds are typically capped around 11% or 13%. This means the maximum you can make every year is the cap (also known as ceiling). And, it gets better! Every ceiling has a floor, so when the index loses money in a given year, you don't incur a loss. Your accumulated wealth remains at the floor for that year, unharmed. Some Life Insurance companies raise the floor to 1% growth during a negative year. Either way, people who invest their Life Insurance through an Index, could typically see a 7%-9% return. It's both a safe and profitable way to accumulate Tax-Free Wealth for retirement.

Many CEOs of Fortune 500 Companies choose Life Insurance primarily because there are no income limitations to qualify. Their earned income is simply too high for the rules of a Roth IRA. The same goes for most doctors, lawyers, and successful business owners. They most often choose to put their money in Life Insurance to attain a Tax-Free retirement.

Death Benefit

Even more advantages are found in Life Insurance over a Roth IRA. In case of death, your Beneficiaries could receive 20-30 times the amount of money invested. While in a Roth IRA, your Beneficiaries receive whatever value has accumulated in the account balance up to that point. In both Life Insurance and Roth IRA, your beneficiaries can receive the money Tax-Free.

When it comes to Life Insurance, it's important to note the value of the Death Benefit begins on the Effective Date of your Policy. Let's say Tom has a Life Insurance Policy where he pays $20,000/year with a Death Benefit of $2 Million. Suddenly he suffers an early death in Year 2. It is horrible to think about it, but death happens.

However, his loved ones are at ease financially, because they receive $2 Million Tax-Free from his Death

Benefit. He only invested $40,000 over 2 years before his early death. Had he done a Roth IRA instead, with the same $40,000 invested over 2 years, how much would his beneficiaries received? Not much… maybe $50,000 or whatever little it has grown to by that point. Either way, there's a big difference between $2,000,000 and $50,000… right?

Long-Term Care

We are fortunate to have modern medicine take bigger strides every year. This has lead to longer lives for many of us. However, long-term care is a reality some of us will need, as we face the twilight of our years. Many Life Insurance companies have a provision that allows you to take proceeds from your death benefit to pay for long-term care (should the need arise). You may be thinking you don't really need it, but consider this:

Let's say a few years into retirement at age 72, you suffer an illness that severely impairs you to perform normal tasks, and now you need to be placed in a nursing home. Long-term care is now needed but you don't have any insurance bought for this unknown circumstance. From where will the money come?

Let's also say you have an IRA, a pension, and Social Security. A portion of these assets will have to be appropriated to cover your long-term care (as required by the government). It would be a major inconvenience to see these funds dwindle down if you wanted to pass them on to your beneficiary.

Had you done a Life Insurance, you could have taken whatever you needed from the Death Benefit without any hassle to your assets. Some would opt for a separate Long-Term Care Insurance, which would not be wise because you pay premiums on something you may not need. With Life Insurance, your premiums won't be wasted because you have the option to take money from the Death Benefit, should you need it for long-term care.

NO Contribution Limits

Remember, there are contribution limits to a Roth IRA. The annual Roth IRA limit is $6,000 (or $7,000 if you're aged 50 or older). Your earned income must also fall under a certain level. For single filers, your income must be under $122,000; and for married couples filing jointly, that income must be under $193,000. In a nutshell, you are limited even if you qualify for a Roth IRA.

Now let's look at the alternative. With Life

Insurance, it does not matter how much income you make. On top of that, you can make additional contributions from other sources that aren't earned income. It can come from investments, rental income, or other areas. You also are not limited to how much you can contribute. This makes it a very attractive investment for everyone, especially for those with a higher income (CEOs, doctors, lawyers, business owners).

NO Withdrawal Limits

Life is full of surprises when you least expect. It can be difficult to find that extra money to deal with these moments. Fortunately, you get to withdraw from both the Roth IRA and Life Insurance to cover these unexpected costs. However, the Roth IRA comes with rules. If you withdraw before age 59½, a 10% penalty will be assessed.

On the other hand, Life Insurance is amazing! You can withdraw from the policy's Cash Value at any age, with no penalty. And if you need to get creative, there's an extra option to take it as a loan against your policy to pay back later. Life Insurance can also be used as collateral if needed. In a Roth IRA, there's no option to take a loan or have it used as collateral.

Let's Review

There are many other advantages to a Life Insurance policy over a Roth IRA, but the ones we reviewed above are some of the main qualities that make it a great option for your Tax-Free Bucket in retirement.

On the next page is a chart to review these comparisons.

WHERE WILL YOU INVEST?

	ROTH IRA	LIFE INSURANCE
Only Earned Income To Contribute	YES	NO, Invest Any Type of Income
Contribution Limit	$6,000 ($7,000)	UNLIMITED
Earnings Growth	Tax-Free	Tax-Free
Withdrawal	Tax-Free	Tax-Free
Withdrawal Age	After 59 ½	Anytime
Early Withdrawal Penalty	YES, 10%	NO
Asset-Protected	YES	YES
Use As Collateral	NO	YES
Option For Long Term Care	NO	YES
In Case of Death Beneficiaries Get...	Account Balance	Death Benefit, almost 20/30x money invested

Understand, that we are discussing Permanent Life Insurance... NOT Term Insurance. The fundamentals of Permanent Life Insurance are designed to provide coverage for your entire life. As discussed above, it gives a death benefit but can also be used to invest or save money (known as the policy's cash value). As you pay your premiums, you build up cash value.

Conversely, Term Life Insurance limits the coverage to a certain time period. Typically, you choose 10, 20 or 30 years -- hence the word "Term." If your death occurs within the Term, your beneficiaries receive a payout. Term Insurance becomes attractive because of the very low premiums paid compared to other Permanent Life policies.

Unlike Permanent Life Insurance, Term Life does not build any Cash Value account for savings or investment. For this reason, Term Insurance is not part of the Benji Boom Effect. You are basically throwing money away in premiums for a product that doesn't build savings and investment. We want to keep your money in something that can both grow for you, and still be passed down to your beneficiaries. That is why Permanent Life Insurance is recommended.

Despite all this helpful information, some of you may have some misgivings about Life Insurance. It's understandable, because once again it is ingrained in our psyches that Life Insurance is bad. Yet some of you didn't know the many functions of Life Insurance, especially as a long-term investment that protects your assets. I'm here to tell you that Life Insurance is fantastic!

Consider this, Bank of America owns tax-free assets in the form of Life Insurance at around $22 Billion on their June 2018 Balance Sheet. Wells Fargo similarly does the same at around $18 Billion as of 2018.[2] What does this tell you, if banks are willing to place so much of this into their executives?

Life Insurance is an incredibly stable investment for its Cash Value, which can be hedged to offset any unforeseen financial failure. Banks are savvy when it comes to stable investments. Wouldn't it be wise to focus our investing in the same way?

---

2 Information publicly found at www.fdic.gov

Your Final Provision Is Provisional

Almost there to the end, but you forgot one last hurdle… Provisional Income. What is it? It's a measure the IRS uses to determine how much is taxable on your Social Security benefits. This is a big thing that gets overlooked when people plan for their retirement. Basically, the level of your Provisional Income determines the level of tax on your Social Security Income. The Provisional Income is typically calculated by the sum of:

- Gross Income
- 1099 Form & Interest from Taxable Investments
- All Distributions from Tax-Deferred Bucket (401k, IRAs)
- Employment Income
- Rental Income
- Tax-Free Interest (mostly Municipal Bonds)

  PLUS

- 50% of Social Security Income

This sum total of Provisional Income falls within the threshold listed below, to determine how much Social Security Income should be taxed:

PROVISIONAL INCOME
Married

Provisional Income	Percent of Social Security Subject To Tax
Under $32,000	0%
$32,000 to $44,000	up to 50%
Over $44,000	up to 85%

PROVISIONAL INCOME
Single

Provisional Income	Percent of Social Security Subject To Tax
Under $25,000	0%
$25,000 to $34,000	up to 50%
Over $34,000	up to 85%

To better illustrate, let's say Mike and Naomi have begun their retirement years. They figure $100,000/year is a good number to live comfortably in retirement and maintain their quality of lifestyle. In order to reach this number, they take a combined $30,000 in Social Security Benefits + $10,000 a year from municipal bonds + $60,000 in 401(k).

1. Withdrawal 401(k)	$60,000
2. Municipal Bonds	$10,000
3. Half of Social Security ($30,000)	+ $15,000
	$85,000 Provisional Income

Percent of Social Security Subject to Tax: 85%

$30,000 Soc. Security

x 85%

$25,500 → $25,500

x 22% Tax Rate

$5,610 Tax Owed

Unfortunately, they forgot about Uncle Sam knocking on the door to collect his share. He's all about calculating Provisional Income... 50% of $30,000 Social Security equals $15,000. Add that to $70,000 (from bonds and 401k) and they get a Provisional Income of $85,000.

73

This number is over $44,000 , which means 85% of Social Security is subject to be taxed (in this case $30,000). So they multiply 85% x $30,000 to get the Amount of Taxable Social Security = $25,500.

Next, they determine their highest level of Tax Rate based on $100,000/year to be 22%. So they multiply $25,500 x 22% to get Social Security Tax = $5,610.

And guess what? They're both angry, because they have to pay this extra tax. Now they're scratching their heads, trying to figure out how to minimize this extra Social Security Tax (it comes every year). They consider taking much less from their 401(k), in order to lower their Provisional Income and reduce Social Security Tax.

But here's the dilemma they now face with their 401(k):

1. Take the Required Minimum Distribution of $60,000 and pay Social Security Tax

--OR--

2. Take less than the Required Minimum Distribution and pay 50% Penalty

In other words, if they don't take out enough from their 401(k), they incur a 50% Penalty. If they take out too much, they lose to Social Security Tax. *What if they had just put that money in the Tax-Free Bucket instead?* They would neither be constrained to the rules of RMD (Required Minimum Distribution), nor constrained to paying Social Security Tax. They could literally pay ZERO in Social Security Tax, because their Provisional Income would be under $32,000. Plus, they can take money from their Tax-Free Bucket with no hassle (to maintain their $100,000/year lifestyle).

Also, let's not forget, there are taxes to be paid on an IRA or 401(k) because it's Tax-Deferred. This is on top of the Social Security Tax! We discussed earlier, that Federal Income Taxes are very likely to go up in the future. So why place the burden of unnecessary tax in retirement?

A Final Word Of Provision

Look up the word *Provisional* in the dictionary. It literally means something that exists in the present, but can possibly be changed later. How much faith do you have in a system whose current rules exist for the time being? I don't want to scare you, but just take a moment to understand the gray area of this term. The word in itself, functions to give Uncle Sam full control over how much he takes (both now and in the future).

In other words...

pay your taxes NOW, not later!!

A New Mindset

In the past, old thinking grounded us into believing that we must look for investments with a higher rate of return in order to achieve higher wealth. That's unnecessary risk now that we have the power of the Benji Boom Effect. By reigning in the Benji's that we leak, combined with the tax savings shifted to our Tax-Free Bucket, we can enjoy a prosperous retirement that maintains our current lifestyle... with no stress.

Compound Interest Makes More Than Cents

Let me repeat that...

Compound Interest makes more than cents.

It is the 8th Wonder of the World. You will see it as a powerful investment tool in the Tax-Free Bucket. The image above represents this concept for Step 3's BOOM!

To better understand, let's first define **Interest**: Payment from a deposit-taking financial entity to the depositor of an amount above repayment of the principal sum (the amount borrowed), at a defined rate of return.

For the purpose of this book, we are depositing Benji's into the Tax-Free Bucket, so that we may withdraw even more Benji's than we originally deposited.

Simple Interest vs. Compound Interest

Understanding the difference between Simple Interest vs. Compound Interest will make you smarter in matters of money. Rather than go into much detail, we'll simplify the concepts:

Simple Interest
- Calculated on the Principal portion in the account.
- Interest = Principal x Interest Rate x Term.
- Typically found in basic loans, not investments.

Compound Interest
- Calculated on Principal and Accumulated Interest.
- This combined formula is commonly known as *"Interest On Interest"*

Compound Interest In Action

To illustrate, let's say you've done a good job to *Find* the money, and have come up with an extra $1,000 set aside into the Tax-Free Bucket. Let's map it out over a 10-year period and assume an 8% rate of return. We will not put in any extra money and will compound the interest once per year.

Year	Deposit	Previous Year ($)	8% Interest	Total
2020	$1,000	-	$80	$1,080
2021	-	$1,080	$86.40	$1,166.40
2022	-	$1,166.40	$93.31	$1,259.71
2023	-	$1,259.71	$100.78	$1,360.49
2024	-	$1,360.49	$108.84	$1,469.33
2026	-	$1,469.33	$117.54	$1,586.87
2027	-	$1,586.87	$126.95	$1,713.82
2028	-	$1,713.82	$137.11	$1,850.93
2029	-	$1,850.93	$148.07	$1,999.00
2030	-	$1,999.00	$159.92	$2,158.92

Deposit + Previous Year ($) + 8% Interest = Total

See how well your $1,000 deposit grew? It more than doubled to $2,158.92 due to compound interest. Now let's say you put an additional $1,000 every year... Your Benji's will BOOM to $17,804.41 from compound interest!

Double Your Penny Over 30 Days

To illustrate compound interest in the simplest way, if I offer you a choice between $1 Million or Double Your Penny Over 30 Days, which would you choose?

It's best to Double Your Penny! Take a look:

BOOM!

Day 1	$0.01
2	$0.02
3	$0.04
4	$0.08
5	$0.16
6	$0.32
7	$0.64
8	$1.28
9	$2.56
10	$5.12
11	$10.24
12	$20.48
13	$40.96
14	$81.92
15	$163.84
16	$327.68
17	$655.36
18	$1,310.72
19	$2,621.44
20	$5,242.88
21	$10,485.76
22	$20,971.52
23	$41,943.04
24	$83,886.08
25	$167,772.16
26	$335,544.32
27	$671,088.64
28	$1,342,177.28
29	$2,684,354.56
Day 30	$5,368,709.12

Of course, there aren't many investment vehicles that double your money in this extreme manner in 30 days. More so, we use this as an example to show the power of compound interest. In the beginning, it will grow slowly, but should you stick with it and not touch that money, your wealth will grow exponentially over the long term.

Why wait? The time is now. The younger you are, the less you need to invest in reaching $1 Million. The older you are, the more difficult it becomes.

Again, this Double Your Penny chart is just an illustration to demonstrate the power of compounding interest as a concept.

However, we must not forget the Power of Uncle Sam. Let's stay with this chart a little longer to illustrate the effects of taxation. If the government taxes 30% for every time you double your penny, then your growth would look something like this:

BOOM!

Day 1	$0.01
2	$0.02
3	$0.03
4	$0.05
5	$0.08
6	$0.14
7	$0.24
8	$0.41
9	$0.70
10	$1.19
11	$2.02
12	$3.43
13	$5.83
14	$9.90
15	$16.84
16	$28.62
17	$48.66
18	$82.72
19	$140.63
20	$239.07
21	$406.42
22	$690.92
23	$1,174.56
24	$1,996.76
25	$3,394.49
26	$5,770.63
27	$9,810.07
28	$16,677.11
29	$28,351.09
Day 30	$48,196.86

Double Your Penny
With & Without Tax

Without Tax	With 30% Tax
$5,368,709.12	$48,196.86

Take a look above at the difference. Do you see the enormous impact taxes play in stunting the potential growth? This happens with most investments, where the growth is taxed each term, before it can grow further into the next term.

Once again, Double Your Penny is just an illustration of a concept, but look at how much taxes can affect your investments. It would greatly benefit you to adjust your strategy to minimize this impact, would it not?

That's why we have the power of the Tax-Free Bucket where we can make our Benji's BOOM without the hassle of Uncle Sam. It's time to fill this bucket now!

This is an important step to The Benji Boom Effect!

STEP 4: **ENJOY**

The Benji Boom Effect

4. Enjoy

Peace Of Mind

You've made it! All the Benji's you've BOOMED have grown to multiples of Benji's for you to enjoy. This step is the simplest one to complete. Most of you will enjoy this part of The Benji Boom Effect in retirement.

Some of you though, will make it hard on yourselves no matter how easy this step, because fear will take over the mind when it comes to spending money. If you have done all the steps right, then you should be able to maintain the same lifestyle you had pre-retirement.

We have eliminated most tax issues in retirement that others will suffer through, because they mismanaged their own planning. You have nothing to fear. The main stuff is covered into your twilight years.

- **Current Lifestyle** – Maintained through Cash Value of your Life Insurance
- **Inheritance** – Passed on to loved ones through the Death Benefit of your Life Insurance

I'm Worried About My Kids

Children become an unnecessary worry for you. Don't hold onto your money for them. I'll give you two reasons why:

1. They will make money in their own life.
2. When you're gone, they will be taken care of by the Death Benefit you leave for them.

So what's the worry? You worked hard leading up to these years, along with patience and commitment, for the health of your wealth. It has BOOMED into an abundance of Benji's for you to enjoy.

SO ENJOY IT!

Put It All Together

Let's make a draft of your blueprint to a better life, starting now. Use it as a reference to map out your strategy. For many of you, this could be an ideal fit to reach a better retirement.

The Heart Of It All

- Review your 4 core values.
- If you are a couple, discuss your values so that you both understand each other's idea of retirement.

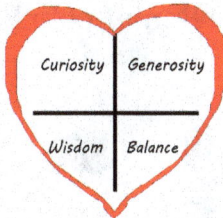

The Benji Boom Effect

- Find the leaks
- Save your money's life
- Make it BOOM!

The Bucket Strategy

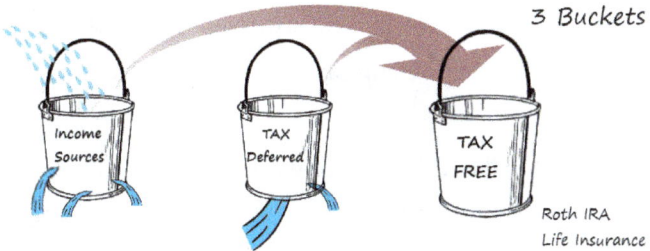

3 Buckets

Income Sources

TAX Deferred

TAX FREE

Roth IRA
Life Insurance

Bucket #1 -- Taxable Income

- **FIND** and plug the leaks.
- Think about how long this bucket will last.

Bucket #2 -- Tax Deferred

- Try to rollover this money to the Tax-Free Bucket.
- Meet with a certified professional to weigh your options... **SAVE** your Benji's from this bucket.

Bucket #3 – Tax-Free

- Consider both Roth IRA and Permanent Life Insurance with a certified professional.
- If feasible, aim for a Provisional Income that keeps your Social Security untaxed.
- Make it **BOOM!**

A Final Note…

- In today's world, a penny saved won't get you much, but a Benji saved will get you far.

- Plug the leaks in your wealth to help you gather loose Benji's.

- You can plant these gathered Benji's, whose seed will grow into trees, which then multiply to vast orchards.

- This is how you make me BOOM!

Keep me with you, don't ever lose me.

Our goal is to bring you closer to a fulfilling retirement.

Always remember...

> ***"A Benji Saved, Is A Benji BOOMED!"***
>
>   - Benji Boom

What Next?

Congratulations on finishing this book! I hope *The Benji Boom Effect* gives you a better blueprint for your financial decisions. The process is simple, but what is next for you?

SCHEDULE AN APPOINTMENT

Email: info@benjiboom.com

Phone: 1.866.800.4771

Now is the best time to review your financial blueprint, while the information we covered is fresh in your mind. We will schedule a call, discuss things on your mind, and then meet up to form a sound financial blueprint for you.

You are also welcome to fill out an online form:

www.benjiboom.com

Thank You!

To Learn More
Visit

www.benjiboom.com

-or-

Instagram
Facebook
Twitter
YouTube

@BenjiBoomEffect

Benji Boom is a character molded from the imagination of Vishal Patel to bring a fun & simple method of understanding wealth. For over 5 years, he has worked closely under the mentor-ship of Ashok Sanghavi, a Certified Financial Planner (C.F.P.) & Chartered Financial Consultant, who passed a C.P.A. He also specializes as a tax strategist. Together, they serve clients across America, specializing in Retirement Planning, Tax Planning & Asset Protection.

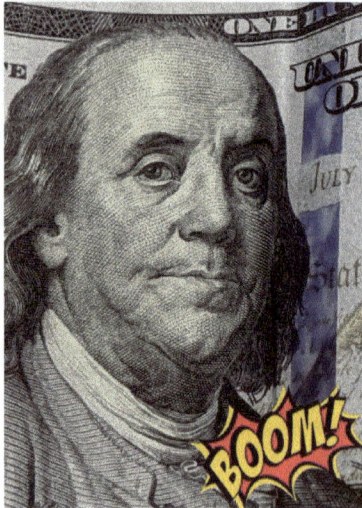

To see more of Benji Boom, check out his YouTube channel where he uncovers more ideas and tips for a greater path to financial stability.